Hug *it* Out

When I was still at home in Michigan, I spent many snowbound evenings crocheting gifts with my mom. Years later, my mom passed away and I was inconsolable. I found myself with too much time on my hands and the grief taking its toll. One day, I saw a link in someone's email to an online group that created afghans to comfort people. All I would have to do is make a twelve-inch square and send it in. It would become part of a full-sized afghan. Now, that I could do!

I began to send in squares. Without realizing it, as I crocheted I kept thinking about my mom and all the good memories I had of her. The motion of working with yarn was the therapy I needed, easing my grief. Truly, if you want to find comfort, give comfort to someone else!

That's why I'm so happy to have created this book of patterns, including afghans, chemo caps, a teddy bear, and a prayer shawl. They will give you the opportunity to help others in their time of need. Giving is the heart and soul of every 'crocheter' I have ever met, without exception!

—*Drew Emborsky*

About The Crochet Dude

Drew Emborsky became known as The Crochet Dude while working with a charity group after the passing of his mother. His time with the group eventually led to his popular blog, which led to the publication of his patterns and guest appearances on HGTV and DIY programs.

men's knit fashion book to several crochet publications of his own, Drew's design career continues to flourish.

Drew lives in Houston, Texas with his cats Chandler and Cleocatra. Catch up with him at thecrochetdude.com and blog.thecrochetdude.com. To see additional Leisure Arts books filled with Drew's must-have projects, visit LeisureArts.com.

I0893626

Table of Contents

LEISURE ARTS, INC.
Little Rock, Arkansas

Mobius Cowl

EASY +

If you would like to make a multipurpose garment for someone who has mobility challenges I have come up with this design just for you. The cowl can be worn several different ways such as over the shoulders, around the neck, and as a hood. This makes it especially easy for the person wearing it to have the right amount of warmth as they go from room to room or inside to outside, and the cowl shape keeps it from falling off the shoulders!

Finished Size: 18" (45.5 cm) wide x 54" (137 cm) circumference

MATERIALS

LIGHT 3

Light Weight Yarn
[5 ounces, 459 yards
(141 grams, 420 meters) per skein]: 2 skeins
Crochet hook, size G (4 mm) **or** size needed for gauge
Marker

GAUGE: 16 hdc and 11 rows/rnds = 4" (10 cm)

Gauge Swatch: 4" (10 cm) square
Ch 18.
Row 1: Hdc in third ch from hook **(2 skipped chs count as first hdc)** and in each ch across: 16 hdc.
Row 2: Ch 2 **(counts as first hdc)**, turn; hdc in Front Loop Only of next hdc and each hdc across ***(Fig. 1, page 26)***.
Row 3: Ch 2, turn; hdc in Back Loop Only of next hdc and each hdc across.
Rows 4-11: Repeat Rows 2 and 3, 4 times.
Finish off.

COWL

Ch 217.

Foundation Rnd (Right side)**:** Hdc in third ch from hook, place marker around st just made, hdc in next ch and in each ch across; rotate piece so beginning ch is facing up then bring marked hdc to meet last hdc made, working in free loops of beginning ch ***(Fig. 2, page 26)***, hdc in ch at base of marked hdc (forms twist) and in each ch across, do **not** join: 430 hdc.

Rnd 1: Hdc in Front Loop Only of marked hdc ***(Fig. 1, page 26)***, move marker to hdc just made to mark beginning of round, hdc in Front Loop Only of next hdc and each hdc around.

Rnds 2-21: Hdc in Front Loop Only of marked hdc, move marker to hdc just made, hdc in Front Loop Only of next hdc and each hdc around.

Rnd 22: Working in Back Loops Only ***(Fig. 1, page 26)***, ★ dc in next hdc, (dc, ch 2, sc in second ch from hook, dc) in next hdc; repeat from ★ around; join with slip st to first dc, finish off.

Chemo Cap

EASY

As someone undergoes treatment for cancer and other illnesses and lose their hair, the right cap can make such a difference. The hat should be as soft as possible because of skin sensitivity, be very comfortable to sleep in, and a little fluffy is nice to visually compensate for the thickness that is lost when there is no hair underneath. I believe these hats do all of that and I even made some modifications so that the man's hat has a trendy skullcap look to it, and the ladies hat has some cute details.

Size	Finished Measurements
Men's	21" circumference x 8" tall (53.5 cm x 20.5 cm)
Women's	19" circumference x 11" tall (48.5 cm x 28.5 cm)

Size Note: Instructions are written for Men's size with Women's size in braces { }. Instructions will be easier to read if you circle all the numbers pertaining to your size. If only one number is given, it applies to both sizes.

MATERIALS

SUPER BULKY 6

Super Bulky Weight Yarn
[3 ounces, 35 yards
(85 grams, 32 meters) per skein]:
2 skeins
Crochet hook, size L (8 mm) **or** size needed for gauge
Yarn needle

GAUGE: In pattern,
(dc, ch 1) 4 times and 4 rows = 4" (10 cm)

Gauge Swatch: 3½"w x 4"h (9 cm x 10 cm)
Ch 10.
Work same as Cap through Row 4.
Finish off.

Each row is worked across the height of the Cap.

BODY

Leaving a long end for sewing, ch 20{26}.

Row 1 (Right side)**:** Dc in sixth ch from hook **(5 skipped chs count as first dc plus ch 1 and one skipped ch)**, ★ ch 1, skip next ch, dc in next ch; repeat from ★ across: 9{12} dc and 8{11} ch-1 sps.

Note: Loop a short piece of yarn around any stitch to mark Row 1 as **right** side.

Rows 2 thru 21{19}: Ch 4 **(counts as first dc plus ch 1)**, turn; dc in next dc, ★ ch 1, skip next ch-1 sp, dc in next dc; repeat from ★ across.

Finish off, leaving a long end for sewing.

FINISHING

Thread yarn needle with either end. With **wrong** side together and working in free loops of beginning ch ***(Fig. 2, page 26)*** and sts on last row, whipstitch Body together, forming a tube ***(Fig. 4, page 26)***.

Thread yarn needle with remaining end. Weave yarn through ends of rows on one edge of Body; gather **tightly** and secure end.

For Women's Cap, weave a length of yarn through first 6 sts at bottom edge of Cap; pull **tightly** to gather and secure ends.

Baby Comfort Blanket

EASY

Check with your local hospital, family shelter, women's center, or child advocacy group to see what needs they have. Swaddling a baby in a handmade blanket can bring comfort to everyone. This ruffled little blanket I've designed would make any baby very happy.

Finished Size: 25¾"w x 33"h (65.5 cm x 84 cm) (excluding ruffle)

MATERIALS

MEDIUM 4

Medium Weight Yarn
[4 ounces, 203 yards
(113 grams, 186 meters) per skein]:
- Blue - 3 skeins
- Pink - 2 skeins

Crochet hook, size H (5 mm) **or** size needed for gauge

GAUGE: In pattern,
18 sts and 16 rows = 4" (10 cm)

Gauge Swatch: 4¼" x 4" (12.75 cm x 10 cm)
With Blue, ch 20.
Work same as Body through Row 18: 10 sc and 9 ch-1 sps.
Finish off.

Each row is worked across the length of the Body.

BODY

With Pink, ch 118.

Row 1 (Wrong side)**:** Sc in second ch from hook, ★ ch 1, skip next ch, sc in next ch; repeat from ★ across: 59 sc and 58 ch-1 sps.

Note: Loop a short piece of yarn around the **back** of any stitch on Row 1 to mark **right** side.

Row 2: Ch 1, turn; sc in first sc and in next ch-1 sp, ★ ch 1, skip next sc, sc in next ch-1 sp; repeat from ★ across to last sc, sc in last sc: 60 sc and 57 ch-1 sps.

Row 3: Ch 1, turn; sc in first sc, ch 1, ★ skip next sc, sc in next ch-1 sp, ch 1; repeat from ★ across to last 2 sc, skip next sc, sc in last sc: 59 sc and 58 ch-1 sps.

Rows 4-8: Repeat Rows 2 and 3 twice, then repeat Row 2 once **more**.

Row 9: Ch 1, turn; sc in first sc and in each sc and each ch-1 sp across: 117 sc.

Row 10: Ch 1, turn; sc in first sc, ★ ch 1, skip next sc, sc in next sc; repeat from ★ across: 59 sc and 58 ch-1 sps.

Rows 11-16: Repeat Rows 2 and 3, 3 times.

Row 17: Ch 1, turn; sc in first sc and in each sc and each ch-1 sp across: 117 sc.

Rows 18-73: Repeat Rows 10-17, 7 times; at end of Row 73, finish off.

BORDER

Rnd 1: With **right** side facing, join Blue with sc in first sc on Row 73 ***(see Joining With Sc, page 26)***, ch 2, sc in same st (corner made), ch 1, † (skip next st, sc in next st, ch 1) across to last 2 sts, skip next st, (sc, ch 2, sc) in last st (corner made), ch 1; working in ends of rows, skip first row, (sc in next row, ch 1, skip next row) across †; working in free loops of beginning ch ***(Fig. 2, page 26)***, (sc, ch 2, sc) in same ch as first sc (corner made), repeat from † to † once; join with slip st to first sc: 194 sc and 194 sps.

Rnds 2-7: Slip st in next corner ch-2 sp, ch 1, (sc, ch 2, sc) in same sp, ch 1, skip next sc, ★ † (sc in next ch-1 sp, ch 1, skip next sc) across to next corner ch-2 sp †, (sc, ch 2, sc) in corner ch-2 sp, ch 1, skip next sc; repeat from ★ 2 times **more**, then repeat from † to † once; join with slip st to first sc: 218 sc and 218 sps.

Rnd 8: Slip st in next corner ch-2 sp, ch 1, (sc, ch 2, sc) in same sp, sc in next sc and in each sc and each ch-1 sp across to next corner ch-2 sp, ★ (sc, ch 2, sc) in corner ch-2 sp, sc in next sc and in each sc and ch-1 sp across; repeat from ★ 2 times **more**; join with slip st to first sc: 440 sc and 4 ch-2 sps.

Rnd 9: Slip st in next corner ch-2 sp, ch 1, (sc, ch 2, sc) in same sp, ch 1, skip next sc, (sc in next sc, ch 1, skip next sc) across to next corner ch-2 sp, ★ (sc, ch 2, sc) in corner ch-2 sp, ch 1, skip next sc, (sc in next sc, ch 1, skip next sc) across to next corner ch-2 sp; repeat from ★ 2 times **more**; join with slip st to first sc: 226 sc and 226 sps.

Rnds 10-15: Repeat Rnds 2-7: 250 sc and 250 sps.

Rnd 16 (Ruffle)**:** (Slip st, ch 1, 3 sc) in next corner ch-2 sp, sc in each sc and in each ch-1 sp around working 3 sc in each corner ch-2 sp; join with slip st to first sc: 508 sc.

Rnd 17: Ch 3 **(counts as first dc)**, dc in same st, 2 dc in next sc and in each sc around; join with slip st to first dc.

Rnd 18: Ch 1, sc in same st, ch 1, (sc in next dc, ch 1) around; join with slip st to first sc, finish off.

Kennel Blanket

EASY

Many pets are dropped off or found abandoned and taken to a local shelter. These pets often spend a long time in kennels with cold hard floors. Reach out to your local humane society, shelter, or pet rescue groups and see if they would like some crocheted comfort for their animals. I've designed this little (stash buster!) blanket to be pet friendly and easy to wash, sure to help a little dog or cat rest easier as she waits for her forever home.

Finished Size: 28" x 32" (71 cm x 81.5 cm)

MATERIALS

MEDIUM 4

Medium Weight Yarn
[5 ounces, 256 yards
(140 grams, 234 meters) per skein]:
- Tan - 3 skeins
- Rust - 1 skein
- Green - 1 skein
- Orange - 1 skein
- Blue - 1 skein

Crochet hook, size H (5 mm) **or** size needed for gauge

GAUGE: In pattern,
13 sts and 8 rows = 4" (10 cm)

Gauge Swatch: 4" (10 cm) square
With Tan, ch 16.
Work same as Blanket for 8 rows: 13 sc.

STITCH GUIDE

LINKED DOUBLE CROCHET *(abbreviated Ldc)*
Insert hook in side of last st made ***(Fig. A)***, YO and pull up a loop, insert hook in next st, YO and pull up a loop (3 loops on hook), (YO and draw through 2 loops on hook) twice.

Fig. A

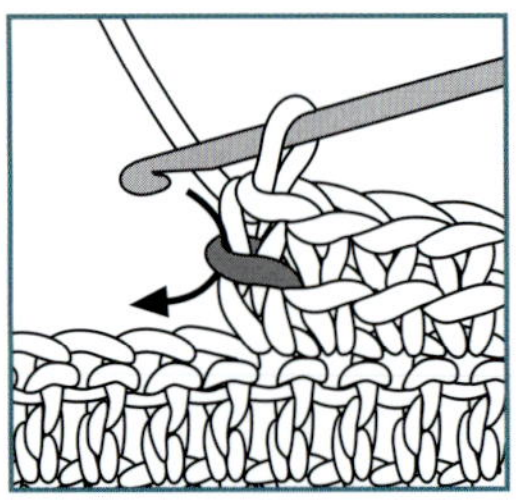

BLANKET

Note: Each row is worked across the length of the Blanket with **right** side facing throughout.

With Tan, ch 108, place marker in fourth ch from hook for st placement.

Row 1 (Right side)**:** Insert hook in second ch from hook, YO and pull up a loop, skip next ch, insert hook in marked ch, YO and pull up a loop (3 loops on hook), (YO and draw through 2 loops on hook) twice (first Ldc made), work Ldc in next ch and in each ch across; finish off: 105 Ldc.

Note: Loop a short piece of yarn around any stitch to mark Row 1 as **right** side.

Row 2: Working in Back Loops Only ***(Fig. 1, page 26)***, join Rust with sc in first Ldc ***(see Joining With Sc, page 26)***; sc in each Ldc across; finish off.

Row 3: Working in Back Loops Only, join Tan with dc in first sc ***(see Joining With Dc, page 26)***; work Ldc in next sc and in each sc across; finish off.

Row 4: Working in Back Loops Only, join Green with sc in first st; sc in each st across; finish off.

Row 5: Working in Back Loops Only, join Tan with dc in first st; work Ldc in each st across; finish off.

Row 6: With Orange, repeat Row 4.

Row 7: Repeat Row 5.

Row 8: With Blue, repeat Row 4.

Rows 9-11: Repeat Row 5, 3 times.

Row 12: With Rust, repeat Row 4.

Rows 13-15: Repeat Row 5, 3 times.

Row 16: Repeat Row 4.

Rows 17-19: Repeat Row 5, 3 times.

Row 20: With Orange, repeat Row 4.

Rows 21-23: Repeat Row 5, 3 times.

Row 24: With Blue, repeat Row 4.

Rows 25-27: Repeat Row 5, 3 times.

Row 28: With Rust, repeat Row 4.

Row 29: Repeat Row 5.

Rows 30-61: Repeat Rows 4-29 once, then repeat Rows 4-9 once **more**.

Baby Hat

EASY

Even the smallest of premature babies benefit from wearing a handmade hat. Be sure to use the very softest yarn possible! Check with your local hospital and see what guidelines they have for donating hats for their preemie babies.

Size	Approximate Finished Circumference & Height
Preemie	
X-Small	5½" x 3½" (14 cm x 9 cm)
Small	6" x 4¼" (15 cm x 11 cm)
Medium	7" x 4¼" (18 cm x 11 cm)
Large	8" x 5" (20.5 cm x 12.5 cm)
X-Large	9" x 6" (23 cm x 15 cm)
Full-term	10½" x 6½" (26.5 cm x 16.5 cm)

Size Note: Instructions are written with Preemie sizes X-Small, Small and Medium in the first set of braces { } and with Preemie sizes Large, X-Large and size Full-term in the second set of braces. Instructions will be easier to read if you circle all the numbers pertaining to your child's size. If only one number is given, it applies to all sizes.

MATERIALS

MEDIUM 4

Medium Weight Yarn
[4 ounces, 203 yards
(113 grams, 186 meters) per skein]:
1 skein
Crochet hook, size I (5.5 mm) **or** size needed for gauge
Yarn needle

GAUGE: In pattern,
18 sts and 15 rows = 4" (10 cm)

Gauge Swatch: 4¼" wide x 4" high
(10.75 cm x 10 cm)

Ch 20.

Row 1: Sc in second ch from hook, ★ ch 1, skip next ch, sc in next ch; repeat from ★ across: 10 sc and 9 ch-1 sps.

Row 2: Ch 1, turn; sc in first sc and in next ch-1 sp, ★ ch 1, skip next sc, sc in next ch-1 sp; repeat from ★ across to last sc, sc in last sc: 11 sc and 8 ch-1 sps.

Row 3: Ch 1, turn; sc in first sc, ch 1, ★ skip next sc, sc in next ch-1 sp, ch 1; repeat from ★ across to last 2 sc, skip next sc, sc in last sc: 10 sc and 9 ch-1 sps.

Rows 4-15: Repeat Rows 2 and 3, 6 times.

Finish off.

Each row is worked across the height of the Hat.

HAT

Ch {16-20-20}{24-28-30}.

Row 1 (Right side)**:** Sc in second ch from hook, ★ ch 1, skip next ch, sc in next ch; repeat from ★ across: {8-10-10}{12-14-15} sc and {7-9-9}{11-13-14} ch-1 sps.

Note: Loop a short piece of yarn around any stitch to mark Row 1 as **right** side.

Row 2: Ch 1, turn; sc in first sc and in next ch-1 sp, ★ ch 1, skip next sc, sc in next ch-1 sp; repeat from ★ across to last sc, sc in last sc: {9-11-11}{13-15-16} sc and {6-8-8}{10-12-13} ch-1 sps.

Row 3: Ch 1, turn; sc in first sc, ch 1, ★ skip next sc, sc in next ch-1 sp, ch 1; repeat from ★ across to last 2 sc, skip next sc, sc in last sc: {8-10-10}{12-14-15} sc and {7-9-9}{11-13-14} ch-1 sps.

Rows 4 thru {20-22-26}{30-34-40}: Repeat Rows 2 and 3, {8-9-11}{13-15-18} times; then repeat Row 2 once **more**.

Finish off, leaving a long end for sewing.

Thread yarn needle with long end. With **wrong** side facing, sew beginning ch to last row to form a tube. Weave needle through ends of rows on edge of tube; gather **tightly** and secure end.

Fold brim up.

Comfortghan

INTERMEDIATE

I spent several years crocheting comfortghan squares, spreading the love and comfort that only handmade can bring. Then one day I broke my foot cooking and the crochet group I worked with sent me a comfortghan! I was so surprised, but more importantly at that moment I realized the true power behind these amazing afghans. I could literally feel the love and joy that went in each stitch of that afghan and I cherish it to this day.

You too can make comfortghans by creating an afghan yourself, or with a group of stitchers. Each of you make a block, using any pattern as long as they all come out 12" (30.5 cm) square, then use the joining method I provided below to stitch them together in a 3 x 4 grid and add the border. Have each stitcher attach a little card sending good thoughts and well-wishes to the square that they made and get ready to get out the tissues as you present the recipient their very own comfortghan.

I've designed an afghan square for you that is quick to make and looks good with any medium weight yarn. Here's a little hint: when you change colors or finish a square be sure to leave a long tail [about 6" (15 cm)] and weave it in back and forth on the wrong side of the afghan – that way the recipient can keep (and wash) the comfortghan for years without the stitches coming apart!

Finished Size: 38" x 50" (96.5 cm x 127 cm)

MATERIALS

MEDIUM 4

Medium Weight Yarn
[5 ounces, 256 yards
(140 grams, 234 meters) per skein]:
Brown **and** Ecru - 3 skeins **each** color
[4 ounces, 204 yards
(113 grams, 187 meters) per skein]:
Variegated - 3 skeins
Crochet hook, size H (5 mm) **or** size needed for gauge

GAUGE SWATCH: 4" (10 cm) square
Work same as Square #1 through Rnd 4.

STITCH GUIDE

TREBLE CROCHET (abbreviated tr)
YO twice, insert hook in st indicated, YO and pull up a loop (4 loops on hook), (YO and draw through 2 loops on hook) 3 times.

PLACEMENT DIAGRAM

FIRST STRIP	SECOND STRIP	THIRD STRIP
#1	#5	#9
#2	#6	#10
#3	#7	#11
#4	#8	#12

Point A (top right corner)

FIRST STRIP

SQUARE #1

Rnd 1 (Right side)**:** With Variegated, ch 4, 15 dc in fourth ch from hook **(3 skipped chs count as first dc)**; join with slip st to first dc: 16 dc.

Note: Loop a short piece of yarn around any stitch to mark Rnd 1 as **right** side.

Rnd 2: Ch 3 **(counts as first dc, now and throughout)**, dc in same st, ch 2, skip next dc, ★ 2 dc in next dc, ch 2, skip next dc; repeat from ★ around; join with slip st to first dc: 16 dc and 8 ch-2 sps.

Rnd 3: Ch 1, sc in same st and in next dc, 2 sc in next ch-2 sp, (sc in next 2 dc, 2 sc in next ch-2 sp) around; join with slip st to first sc: 32 sc.

Rnd 4: Ch 3, dc in next sc, ch 5, skip next 2 sc, ★ dc in next 2 sc, ch 5, skip next 2 sc; repeat from ★ around; join with slip st to first dc: 16 dc and 8 ch-5 sps.

Rnd 5: Ch 1, sc in same st and in next dc, 5 sc in next ch-5 sp, (sc in next 2 dc, 5 sc in next ch-5 sp) around; join with slip st to first sc: 56 sc.

Rnd 6: Ch 3, (dc in next sc, ch 2, skip next sc) 3 times, ★ dc in next 2 sc, ch 2, skip next sc, (dc in next sc, ch 2, skip next sc) twice; repeat from ★ around; join with slip st to first dc: 32 dc and 24 ch-2 sps.

Rnd 7: Ch 1, sc in same st, (sc in next dc, 2 sc in next ch-2 sp) 3 times, ★ sc in next 2 dc, 2 sc in next ch-2 sp, (sc in next dc, 2 sc in next ch-2 sp) twice; repeat from ★ around; join with slip st to first sc: 80 sc.

Rnd 8: Ch 4 **(counts as first tr, now and throughout)**, (tr, ch 3, 2 tr) in same st, ★ † tr in next sc, dc in next 2 sc, hdc in next 2 sc, sc in next 4 sc, 2 sc in next sc, sc in next 4 sc, hdc in next 2 sc, dc in next 2 sc, tr in next sc †, (2 tr, ch 3, 2 tr) in next sc; repeat from ★ 2 times **more**, then repeat from † to † once; join with slip st to first tr: 96 sts and 4 corner ch-3 sps.

Rnd 9: Slip st in next tr and in next corner ch-3 sp, ch 3, (dc, ch 2, 2 dc) in same sp, ch 2, ★ † skip next tr, dc in next 2 tr, ch 2, skip next 2 dc, (dc in next st, ch 2, skip next 2 sts) twice, dc in next 2 sc, ch 2, skip next 2 sc, (dc in next st, ch 2, skip next 2 sts) twice, dc in next 2 tr, ch 2, skip next tr †, (2 dc, ch 2) twice in next corner ch-3 sp; repeat from ★ 2 times **more**, then repeat from † to † once; join with slip st to first dc: 56 dc and 36 ch-2 sps.

Rnd 10: Slip st in next dc and in next corner ch-2 sp, ch 1, 3 sc in same sp, ★ † (sc in next 2 dc, 2 sc in next ch-2 sp) twice, (sc in next dc, 2 sc in next ch-2 sp) twice, sc in next 2 dc, (2 sc in next ch-2 sp, sc in next dc) twice, (2 sc in next ch-2 sp, sc in next 2 dc) twice †, 3 sc in next corner ch-2 sp; repeat from ★ 2 times **more**, then repeat from † to † once; join with slip st to first sc: 132 sc.

Rnd 11: Slip st in next sc, ch 3, (dc, ch 2, 2 dc) in same st, ★ † ch 1, skip next sc, (dc in next 2 sc, ch 2, skip next 2 sc) twice, (dc in next sc, ch 2, skip next 2 sc) twice, dc in next 2 sc, (ch 2, skip next 2 sc, dc in next sc) twice, (ch 2, skip next 2 sc, dc in next 2 sc) twice, ch 1, skip next sc †, (2 dc, ch 2, 2 dc) in next sc; repeat from ★ 2 times **more**, then repeat from † to † once; join with slip st to first dc: 72 dc and 44 sps.

Rnd 12: Slip st in next dc and in next corner ch-2 sp, ch 1, 3 sc in same sp, ★ † sc in next 2 dc and in next ch-1 sp, (sc in next 2 dc, 2 sc in next ch-2 sp) twice, (sc in next dc, 2 sc in next ch-2 sp) twice, sc in next 2 dc, (2 sc in next ch-2 sp, sc in next dc) twice, (2 sc in next ch-2 sp, sc in next 2 dc) twice, sc in next ch-1 sp and in next 2 dc †, 3 sc in next corner ch-2 sp; repeat from ★ 2 times **more**, then repeat from † to † once; join with slip st to first sc: 156 sc.

Rnd 13: Slip st in next sc, ch 3, (dc, ch 2, 2 dc) in same st, ★ † ch 1, skip next sc, dc in next 2 sc, ch 1, skip next sc, (dc in next 2 sc, ch 2, skip next 2 sc) twice, (dc in next sc, ch 2, skip next 2 sc) twice, dc in next 2 sc, (ch 2, skip next 2 sc, dc in next sc) twice, (ch 2, skip next 2 sc, dc in next 2 sc) twice, ch 1, skip next sc, dc in next 2 sc, ch 1, skip next sc †, (2 dc, ch 2, 2 dc) in next sc; repeat from ★ 2 times **more**, then repeat from † to † once; join with slip st to first dc: 88 dc and 52 sps.

Rnd 14: Slip st in next dc and in next corner ch-2 sp, ch 1, 3 sc in same sp, ★ † (sc in next 2 dc and in next ch-1 sp) twice, (sc in next 2 dc, 2 sc in next ch-2 sp) twice, (sc in next dc, 2 sc in next ch-2 sp) twice, sc in next 2 dc, (2 sc in next ch-2 sp, sc in next dc) twice, (2 sc in next ch-2 sp, sc in next 2 dc) twice, (sc in next ch-1 sp and in next 2 dc) twice †, 3 sc in next corner ch-2 sp; repeat from ★ 2 times **more**, then repeat from † to † once; join with slip st to first sc, finish off: 180 sc.

Rnd 15: With **right** side facing, join Ecru with sc in center sc of any corner 3-sc group ***(see Joining With Sc, page 26)***; ch 4, sc in same st, ch 3, skip next 2 sc, (sc in next sc, ch 3, skip next 2 sc) 14 times, ★ (sc, ch 4, sc) in next sc, ch 3, skip next 2 sc, (sc in next sc, ch 3, skip next 2 sc) 14 times; repeat from ★ 2 times **more**; join with slip st to first sc, finish off: 64 sps.

The method used to connect the Squares is a no-sew joining also known as "join-as-you-go". After Square #1 is made, each remaining Square is worked through Rnd 14; then using Placement Diagram, page 12 as a guide, they are crocheted together as Rnd 15 is worked.

SQUARE #2

Rnds 1-7: With Brown, work same as Square #1; at end of Rnd 7, finish off: 80 sc.

Rnd 8: With **right** side facing, join Ecru with slip st in same st as joining; ch 4, (tr, ch 3, 2 tr) in same st, ★ † tr in next sc, dc in next 2 sc, hdc in next 2 sc, sc in next 4 sc, 2 sc in next sc, sc in next 4 sc, hdc in next 2 sc, dc in next 2 sc, tr in next sc †, (2 tr, ch 3, 2 tr) in next sc; repeat from ★ 2 times **more**, then repeat from † to † once; join with slip st to first tr: 96 sts and 4 corner ch-2 sps.

Rnds 9-12: Work same as Square #1; at end of Rnd 12, finish off: 156 sc.

Rnd 13: With **right** side facing, join Variegated with slip st in center sc of any corner 3-sc group; ch 3, (dc, ch 2, 2 dc) in same st, ★ † ch 1, skip next sc, dc in next 2 sc, ch 1, skip next sc, (dc in next 2 sc, ch 2, skip next 2 sc) twice, (dc in next sc, ch 2, skip next 2 sc) twice, dc in next 2 sc, (ch 2, skip next 2 sc, dc in next sc) twice, (ch 2, skip next 2 sc, dc in next 2 sc) twice, ch 1, skip next sc, dc in next 2 sc, ch 1, skip next sc †, (2 dc, ch 2, 2 dc) in next sc; repeat from ★ 2 times **more**, then repeat from † to † once; join with slip st to first dc: 88 dc and 52 sps.

Rnd 14: Work same as Square #1: 180 sc.

Rnd 15 (Joining rnd)**:** With **right** side facing, join Ecru with sc in center sc of any corner 3-sc group; ★ ch 3, skip next 2 sc, (sc in next sc, ch 3, skip next 2 sc) 14 times, (sc, ch 4, sc) in next sc; repeat from ★ 2 times **more**, ch 2; drop loop from hook, with **right** side of **previous Square** facing, insert hook from **front** to **back** in corresponding ch-3 sp, pick up dropped loop, ch 1 (encasing ch-3), skip next 2 sc on **new Square**, † sc in next sc, ch 2, drop loop from hook, insert hook from **front** to **back** in next ch-3 sp on **previous Square**, pick up dropped loop, ch 1 (encasing ch-3), skip next 2 sc on **new Square** †; repeat from † to † 13 times **more**, sc in same st as first sc, ch 4; join with slip st to first sc, finish off: 64 sps.

SQUARE #3

Rnds 1-14: With Brown, work same as Square #1: 180 sc.

Rnd 15 (Joining rnd)**:** Work same as Square #2: 64 sps.

SQUARE #4

Rnds 1-14: Work same as Square #1: 180 sc.

Rnd 15 (Joining rnd)**:** Work same as Square #2: 64 sps.

Instructions continued on page 16.

SECOND STRIP

SQUARE #5

Rnds 1-14: With Ecru, work same as Square #1; do **not** finish off at end of Rnd 14: 180 sc.

Rnd 15 (Joining rnd)**:** Slip st in next sc, ch 1, sc in same st; ★ ch 3, skip next 2 sc, (sc in next sc, ch 3, skip next 2 sc) 14 times, (sc, ch 4, sc) in next sc; repeat from ★ 2 times **more**, ch 2; drop loop from hook, with **right** side of **adjacent Square** facing, insert hook from **front** to **back** in corresponding ch-3 sp, pick up dropped loop, ch 1 (encasing ch-3), skip next 2 sc on **new Square**, † sc in next sc, ch 2, drop loop from hook, insert hook from **front** to **back** in next ch-3 sp on **adjacent Square**, pick up dropped loop, ch 1 (encasing ch-3), skip next 2 sc on **new Square** †; repeat from † to † 13 times **more**, sc in same st as first sc, ch 2, drop loop from hook, insert hook from **front** to **back** in corner ch-4 sp on **diagonal Square**, pick up dropped loop, ch 2 (encasing ch-4); join with slip st to first sc on **new Square**, finish off: 64 sps.

SQUARE #6

Rnds 1-14: With Brown, work same as Square #1: 180 sc.

Rnd 15 (Joining rnd)**:** With **right** side facing, join Ecru with sc in center sc of any corner 3-sc group; ★ ch 3, skip next 2 sc, (sc in next sc, ch 3, skip next 2 sc) 14 times, (sc, ch 4, sc) in next sc; repeat from ★ once **more**, ch 2; drop loop from hook, with **right** side of **adjacent Square** facing, insert hook from **front** to **back** in corresponding ch-3 sp, pick up dropped loop, ch 1 (encasing ch-3), skip next 2 sc on **new Square**, † sc in next sc, ch 2, drop loop from hook, insert hook from **front** to **back** in next ch-3 sp on **adjacent Square**, pick up dropped loop, ch 1 (encasing ch-3), skip next 2 sc on **new Square** †; repeat from † to † 13 times **more**, sc in next sc, ch 2, drop loop from hook, insert hook from **front** to **back** in corner ch-4 sp on **diagonal Square**, pick up dropped loop, ch 2 (encasing ch-4), sc in same st on **new Square**, ch 2, drop loop from hook, insert hook from **front** to **back** in corresponding ch-3 sp on **adjacent Square**, pick up dropped loop, ch 1 (encasing ch-3), skip next 2 sc on **new Square**, repeat from † to † 14 times, sc in same st as first sc, ch 2, drop loop from hook, insert hook from **front** to **back** in corner ch-4 sp on **diagonal Square**, pick up dropped loop, ch 2 (encasing ch-4); join with slip st to first sc on **new Square**, finish off: 64 sps.

SQUARE #7

Rnds 1-7: With Ecru, work same as Square #2: 80 sc.

Rnds 8-12: With Variegated, work same as Square #2: 156 sc.

Rnds 13 and 14: With Brown, work same as Square #2: 180 sc.

Rnd 15 (Joining rnd)**:** Work same as Square #6: 64 sps.

SQUARE #8

Rnds 1-14: With Ecru, work same as Square #1; do **not** finish off at end of Rnd 14: 180 sc.

Rnd 15 (Joining rnd)**: Rnd 15** (Joining rnd)**:** Slip st in next sc, ch 1, sc in same st; ★ ch 3, skip next 2 sc, (sc in next sc, ch 3, skip next 2 sc) 14 times, (sc, ch 4, sc) in next sc; repeat from ★ once **more**, ch 2; drop loop from hook, with **right** side of **adjacent Square** facing, insert hook from **front** to **back** in corresponding ch-3 sp, pick up dropped loop, ch 1 (encasing ch-3), skip next 2 sc on **new Square**, † sc in next sc, ch 2, drop loop from hook, insert hook from **front** to **back** in next ch-3 sp on **adjacent Square**, pick up dropped loop, ch 1 (encasing ch-3), skip next 2 sc on **new Square** †; repeat from † to † 13 times **more**, sc in next sc, ch 2, drop loop from hook, insert hook from **front** to **back** in corner ch-4 sp on **diagonal Square**, pick up dropped loop, ch 2 (encasing ch-4), sc in same st on **new Square**, ch 2, drop loop from hook, insert hook from **front** to **back** in corresponding ch-3 sp on **adjacent Square**, pick up dropped loop, ch 1 (encasing ch-3), skip next 2 sc on **new Square**, repeat from † to † 14 times, sc in same st as first sc, ch 2, drop loop from hook, insert hook from **front** to **back** in corner ch-4 sp on **diagonal Square**, pick up dropped loop, ch 2 (encasing ch-4); join with slip st to first sc on **new Square**, finish off: 64 sps.

THIRD STRIP

SQUARE #9

Rnds 1-7: With Variegated, work same as Square #2: 80 sc.

Rnds 8-12: With Brown, work same as Square #2: 156 sc.

Rnds 13 and 14: With Ecru, work same as Square #2; do **not** finish off at end of Rnd 14: 180 sc.

Rnd 15 (Joining rnd): Work same as Square #5: 64 sps.

SQUARE #10

Rnds 1-14: With Variegated, work same as Square #1: 180 sc.

Rnd 15 (Joining rnd): Work same as Square #6: 64 sps.

SQUARE #11

Work same as Square #8: 64 sps.

SQUARE #12

Work same as Square #6: 64 sps.

BORDER

When working in the unjoined corner ch-4 sps of Squares, overlap the spaces and work through **both** layers.

Rnd 1: With **right** side facing, join Ecru with sc in sc after corner ch-4 sp at Point A ***(see Placement Diagram, page 18)***; ★ † (2 sc in next ch-3 sp, sc in next sc) 15 times, overlap next 2 ch-4 sps to form one ch-4 sp, 2 sc in ch-4 sp, sc in next sc †; repeat from † to † once **more**, (2 sc in next ch-3 sp, sc in next sc) 15 times, 4 sc in next corner ch-4 sp, sc in next sc; repeat from ★ 2 times **more**, then repeat from † to † twice, (2 sc in next ch-3 sp, sc in next sc) 15 times, 4 sc in last corner ch-4 sp; join with slip st to first sc, finish off: 680 sc.

Rnd 2: With **right** side facing and working in Back Loops Only ***(Fig. 1, page 26)***, join Variegated with sc in second sc of any corner 4-sc group; sc in same st, 2 sc in next sc, ★ sc in next sc and in each sc across to second sc of next corner 4-sc group, 2 sc in each of next 2 sc; repeat from ★ 2 times **more**, sc in next sc and in each sc across; join with slip st to first sc, finish off: 688 sc.

Rnd 3: With **right** side facing and working in Back Loops Only, skip same st as joining and join Brown with slip st in next sc; ch 3, dc in same st, 2 dc in next sc, ★ dc in next sc and in each sc across to second sc of next 2-sc group, 2 dc in each of next 2 sc; repeat from ★ 2 times **more**, dc in next sc and in each sc across; join with slip st to first dc, finish off: 696 dc.

Rnd 4: With **right** side facing and working in Back Loops Only, join Ecru with sc in same st as joining; ch 1, sc in top of last sc made ***(Fig. A)***, [sc in next dc, ch 1, sc in top of last sc made] 3 times, skip next dc, ★ ♥ † sc in next dc, ch 1, sc in top of last sc made, skip next dc †; repeat from † to † across to first corner 2-dc group ♥, [sc in next dc, ch 1, sc in top of last sc made] 4 times; repeat from ★ 2 times **more**, then repeat from ♥ to ♥ once; join with slip st to **both** loops of first sc, finish off.

Fig. A

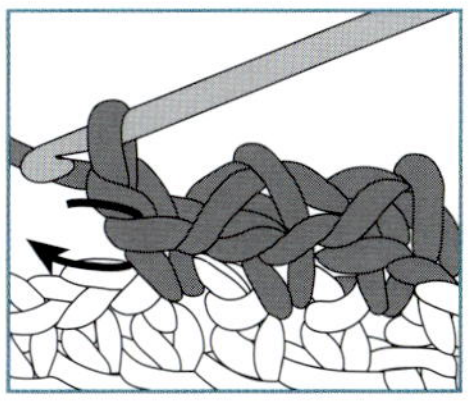

Prayer Shawl

BEGINNER +

This book of crocheting for comfort would not be complete without a pattern for a prayer shawl. What an amazing way to show someone that you are thinking of them and want to comfort them in their time of need. I've designed this shawl so that you can make it with any yarn in your stash, just make each row with a different yarn and be sure to say a little prayer with each stitch or row!

Finished Size: Approximately
66" wide x 24" long at center point
(167.5 cm x 61 cm)
(excluding fringe)

MATERIALS

Medium Weight Yarn (MEDIUM 4)
[3 ounces, 145 yards
(85 grams, 133 meters) per skein]:
Green Variegated - 1 skein
[3 ounces, 103 yards,
(85 grams, 94 meters) per skein]:
Lt Green - 1 skein
Tan - 1 skein
Cream - 1 skein
Bulky Weight Yarn (BULKY 5)
[6 ounces, 185 yards
(170 grams, 169 meters) per skein]:
Blue - 1 skein
Purple - 1 skein
Bulky Weight Novelty Yarn
[1.75 ounces, 64 yards
(50 grams, 58 meters) per ball]:
Ecru - 1 ball
Super Bulky Weight Yarn (SUPER BULKY 6)
[6 ounces, 106 yards
(170 grams, 97 meters) per skein]:
Wine - 1 skein
Crochet hook, size H (5 mm) **or** size needed for gauge

As you mix and match your yarns, start the first row with a medium weight yarn as I have. This will ensure that the beginning size will be correct. Keep using the same size hook for any thickness of yarn and the shawl will turn out great!

Each row is worked with right side facing throughout. When joining yarn and finishing off, leave an 8" (20.5 cm) end to be worked into fringe.

GAUGE: In pattern, 4 V-Sts = 4½" (11.5 cm);
Rows 1-5 = 4" (10 cm)

Gauge Swatch: 4½"w x 4"h (11.5 cm x 10 cm)
With Green Variegated, ch 15.
Row 1 (Right side)**:** Dc in sixth ch from hook **(5 skipped chs count as first dc plus ch 2) (first V-St made)**, (skip next 2 chs, work V-St in next ch) across; finish off: 4 V-Sts.
Rows 2-5: With **right** side facing and following Color Sequence on page 13, join next color with dc in first ch-2 sp ***(see Joining With Dc, page 26)***; ch 2, dc in same sp **(first V-St made)**, work V-St in each of next 3 V-Sts (ch-2 sp); finish off.

STITCH GUIDE

V-STITCH *(abbreviated V-St)*
(Dc, ch 2, dc) in st or sp indicated.

COLOR SEQUENCE

Work one row **each**: ★ † Green Variegated, Blue, Tan, Wine, Cream, Lt Green †, Purple, Ecru; repeat from ★ 2 times **more**, then repeat from † to † once.

With Green Variegated, ch 180.

Row 1 (Right side)**:** Dc in sixth ch from hook **(5 skipped chs count as first dc plus ch 2) (first V-St made)**, (skip next 2 chs, work V-St in next ch) across; finish off: 59 V-Sts.

Note: Loop a short piece of yarn around any stitch to mark Row 1 as **right** side.

Rows 2-29: With **right** side facing, skip first V-St and join next color with dc in next V-St (ch-2 sp) ***(see Joining With Dc, page 26)***, ch 2, dc in same sp; (first V-St made), work V-St in each V-St across leaving last V-St unworked; finish off: 3 V-Sts.

Row 30: With **right** side facing, skip first V-St and join Lt Green with dc in next V-St, ch 2, dc in same sp; finish off leaving last V-St unworked: one V-St.

Instructions continued on page 24.

Comfort Teddy

INTERMEDIATE

When a law enforcement officer shows up to a crime or accident scene they sometimes find frightened children who need more than a hug, they need something to hold on to! This little teddy pulled out of the officer's car and given to a child at the scene can make all the difference in calming the little one down and perhaps ease the trauma just a bit.

Check with your local police station and see if they have a program in place to provide their officers with teddy bears. If not, what a great opportunity you have too start one with them and comfort countless little lives.

Finished Size: 7¾" (19.5 cm) tall

MATERIALS

SUPER FINE 1

- Super Fine Weight Yarn [1.76 ounces, 230 yards (50 grams, 210 meters) per skein]:
  - Brown - 1 skein
  - Cream - small amount
- Crochet hook, size D (3.25 mm) **or** size needed for gauge
- Tapestry needle
- Polyester fiberfill
- Black embroidery floss - small amount

GAUGE: 32 sc and 40 rows/rnds = 4" (10 cm)

Gauge Swatch: 2" (5 cm) square
With Brown, ch 17.
Row 1: Sc in second ch from hook and in each ch across: 16 sc.
Rows 2-20: Ch 1, turn; sc in each sc across.
Finish off.

STITCH GUIDE

DECREASE
Pull up a loop in each of next 2 sc, YO and draw through all 3 loops on hook **(counts as one sc)**.

BEAR

BODY

With Brown, ch 18.

Rnd 1 (Right side)**:** Sc in second ch from hook and in each ch across to last ch, 3 sc in last ch; working in free loops of beginning ch ***(Fig. 2, page 26)***, sc in each ch across to ch at base of first sc, 2 sc in ch at base of first sc, do **not** join, place marker to mark beginning of rnd ***(see Markers, page 26)***: 36 sc.

Rnds 2-22: Sc in each sc around.

Rnd 23: 2 Sc in each sc around: 72 sc.

Rnds 24-56: Sc in each sc around.

Stuff Body with fiberfill.

NECK

Rnd 1: Decrease around: 36 sc.

Rnds 2-7: Sc in each sc around.

HEAD

Rnd 1: (Sc in next sc, 2 sc in next sc) around: 54 sc.

Rnds 2-11: Sc in each sc around.

Rnd 12: Decrease around: 27 sc.

Rnd 13: Sc in next sc, decrease around: 14 sc.

Rnd 14: Decrease around: 7 sc.

Stuff Head with fiberfill.

Rnd 15: Sc in next sc, decrease around; slip st in next sc, finish off leaving a long end for sewing.

Thread tapestry needle with long end. Weave needle through sts and gather **tightly**; secure end.

FINISHING

FIRST EAR

Leaving a long end for sewing, join Brown with dc around sc on Rnd 9 at side of Head ***(see Joining With Dc, page 26)***; 7 dc around same st; finish off leaving a long end for sewing.

SECOND EAR

Leaving a long end for sewing, join Brown with dc around sc on Rnd 9 at opposite side of Head; 7 dc around same st; finish off leaving a long end for sewing.

Thread tapestry needle with either end; sew each edge of Ear to Head. Repeat for remaining Ear.

Instructions continued on page 24.

Drawstring Bag

EASY

Whether it's your school club, your local guild, or your community center, crocheting for a fundraiser is always exciting! I developed this drawstring bag pattern to give you a fun little project that you can finish quickly, you can sell easily, and the best part is you can use up a lot of your partial skeins from other projects!

Finished Size: Approximately 7" tall x 12" circumference (18 cm x 30.5 cm)

MATERIALS

Medium Weight Yarn (MEDIUM 4)
[3.5 ounces, 207 yards
(100 grams, 188 meters) per skein]:
Blue, White, Pink, Purple, Green, and Dk Pink
Each bag uses approximately 80 yards
(73 meters) **total**.
Crochet hook, size I (5.5 mm)
Yarn needle

Gauge is not of great importance; your Bag may be a little larger or smaller without changing the overall effect.

SOLID BAG

Ch 27.

Row 1 (Right side)**:** Sc in second ch from hook and in each ch across: 26 sc.

Note: Loop a short piece of yarn around any stitch to mark Row 1 as **right** side.

Row 2: Ch 1, turn; hdc in Front Loop Only of each sc across ***(Fig. 1, page 26)***.

Row 3: Ch 1, turn; sc in Back Loop Only of each hdc across ***(Fig. 1, page 26)***.

Rows 4-30: Repeat Rows 2 and 3, 13 times; then repeat Row 2 once **more**.

Finish off, leaving a long end for sewing.

STRIPED BAG

Work same as Solid Bag, changing color at end of every other row ***(Fig. 3, page 26)***; at end of Row 24, do **not** change colors.

FINISHING

Thread yarn needle with long end. With **wrong** side together, whipstitch ends together to form a tube ***(Fig. 4, page 26)***, working through free loops of beginning ch ***(Fig. 2, page 26)*** and Back Loop Only of hdc on Row 30. Weave needle through ends of rows on edge of tube; gather **tightly** and secure end.

DRAWSTRING

Chain a 20" (51 cm) length; finish off.

Weave Drawstring through ends of rows at Bag opening.

OPTIONAL HANDLE

Leaving a long end for sewing, chain a 16" (40.5 cm) length; slip st in second ch from hook and in each ch across; finish off leaving a long end for sewing.

Thread yarn needle with either end; sew same end of Handle to inside edge of Bag; repeat for opposite end of Handle.

Prayer Shawl
continued from page 19.

FRINGE
Cut a piece of cardboard 3" (7.5 cm) wide and 8½" (21.5 cm) long. Wind the yarn **loosely** and evenly lengthwise around around the cardboard until you have the amount of strands needed.

Hold together 2 strands of corresponding color yarn of the thicker yarn and 3 to 4 strands of the thinner yarn and fold in half.

With **wrong** side facing and using a crochet hook, draw the folded end up through the first or last V-St on a row and pull the loose ends through the folded end; draw the knot up tightly ***(Figs. A & B)***.

Add additional fringe at the ends of each row across.

Fig. A

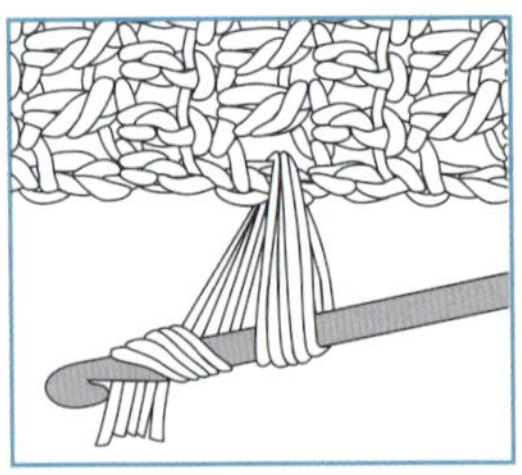

Fig. B

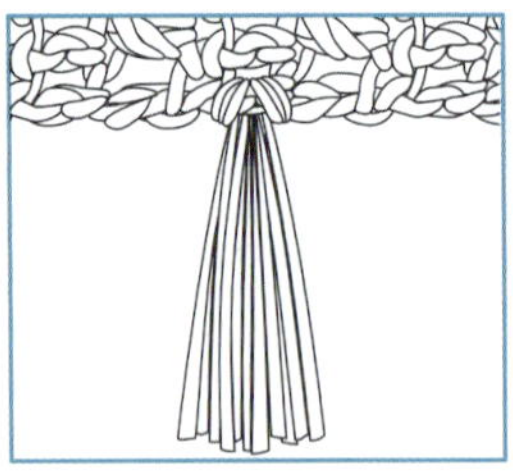

Comfort Teddy
continued from page 21.

SCARF
With Cream, ch 68.

Row 1: Hdc in third ch from hook and in each ch across; finish off.

Thread tapestry needle with an 8" (20.5 cm) length of Brown yarn. Weave through sts on Rnd 3 of Neck, gather and secure ends.

Thread tapestry needle with an 8" (20.5 cm) length of Brown yarn. Beginning at Rnd 1 of Body, sew through both layers to create legs, ending at Rnd 22; secure ends.

Thread tapestry needle with an 8" (20.5 cm) length of Brown yarn. Beginning at either side of Body, sew through both layers to create arms; secure ends. Repeat for opposite side of Body.

Thread tapestry needle with Black floss. Using photo as a guide, embroider satin stitch eyes and nose. Using straight stitch and Cream yarn, add accents around each eye. Using straight stitch and Black floss, add mouth.

Tie scarf around Neck; secure by tacking in place at back of Neck.

SATIN STITCH
Satin Stitch is a series of straight stitches worked side by side so they touch but do not overlap. Come up at odd numbers and go down at even numbers ***(Fig. C)***.

Fig. C

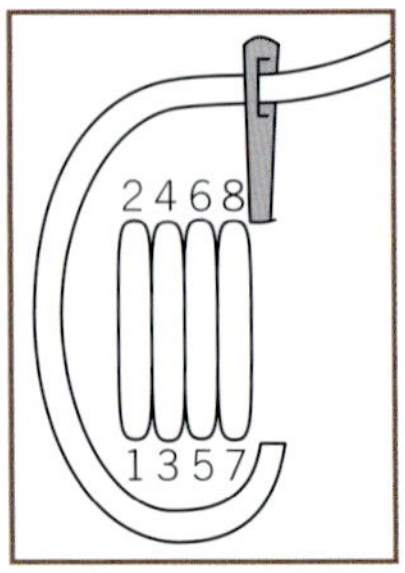

STRAIGHT STITCH
Straight Stitch is just what the name implies, a single, straight stitch. Come up at 1 and go down at 2 ***(Fig. D)***.

Fig. D

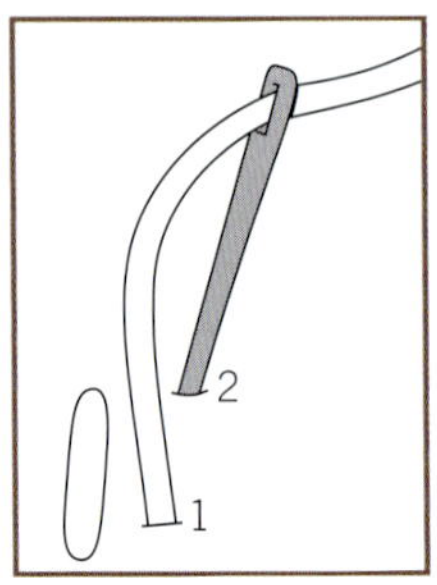

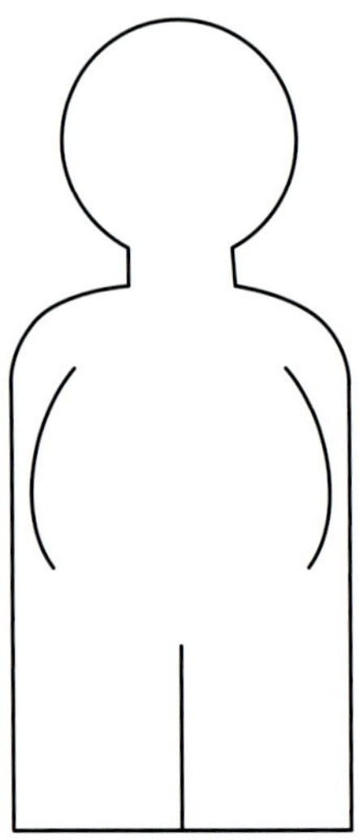

General Instructions

ABBREVIATIONS

ch(s)	chain(s)
cm	centimeters
dc	double crochet(s)
hdc	half double crochet(s)
Ldc	Linked double crochet(s)
mm	millimeters
Rnd(s)	Round(s)
sc	single crochet(s)
sp(s)	space(s)
st(s)	stitch(es)
tr	treble crochet(s)
YO	yarn over

★ — work instructions following ★ as many **more** times as indicated in addition to the first time.

† to † or ♥ to ♥ — work all instructions from first † or ♥ to second † or ♥ **as many** times as specified.

( ) or **[ ]** — work enclosed instructions **as many** times as specified by the number immediately following **or** work all enclosed instructions in the stitch or space indicated **or** contains explanatory remarks.

colon (:) — the number(s) given after a colon at the end of a row or round denote(s) the number of stitches you should have on that row or round.

Yarn Weight Symbol & Names	LACE 0	SUPER FINE 1	FINE 2	LIGHT 3	MEDIUM 4	BULKY 5	SUPER BULKY 6
Type of Yarns in Category	Fingering, 10-count crochet thread	Sock, Fingering Baby	Sport, Baby	DK, Light Worsted	Worsted, Afghan, Aran	Chunky, Craft, Rug	Bulky, Roving
Crochet Gauge* Ranges in Single Crochet to 4" (10 cm)	32-42 double crochets**	21-32 sts	16-20 sts	12-17 sts	11-14 sts	8-11 sts	5-9 sts
Advised Hook Size Range	Steel*** 6,7,8 Regular hook B-1	B-1 to E-4	E-4 to 7	7 to I-9	I-9 to K-10.5	K-10.5 to M-13	M-13 and larger

*GUIDELINES ONLY: The chart above reflects the most commonly used gauges and hook sizes for specific yarn categories.

** Lace weight yarns are usually crocheted on larger-size hooks to create lacy openwork patterns. Accordingly, a gauge range is difficult to determine. Always follow the gauge stated in your pattern.

*** Steel crochet hooks are sized differently from regular hooks–the higher the number the smaller the hook, which is the reverse of regular hook sizing.

CROCHET TERMINOLOGY		
UNITED STATES		**INTERNATIONAL**
slip stitch (slip st)	=	single crochet (sc)
single crochet (sc)	=	double crochet (dc)
half double crochet (hdc)	=	half treble crochet (htr)
double crochet (dc)	=	treble crochet (tr)
treble crochet (tr)	=	double treble crochet (dtr)
double treble crochet (dtr)	=	triple treble crochet (ttr)
triple treble crochet (tr tr)	=	quadruple treble crochet (qtr)
skip	=	miss

BEGINNER	Projects for first-time crocheters using basic stitches. Minimal shaping.
EASY	Projects using yarn with basic stitches, repetitive stitch patterns, simple color changes, and simple shaping and finishing.
INTERMEDIATE	Projects using a variety of techniques, such as basic lace patterns or color patterns, mid-level shaping and finishing.
EXPERIENCED	Projects with intricate stitch patterns, techniques and dimension, such as non-repeating patterns, multi-color techniques, fine threads, small hooks, detailed shaping and refined finishing.

CROCHET HOOKS																
U.S.	B-1	C-2	D-3	E-4	F-5	G-6	H-8	I-9	J-10	K-10½	L-11	M/N-13	N/P-15	P/Q	Q	S
Metric - mm	2.25	2.75	3.25	3.5	3.75	4	5	5.5	6	6.5	8	9	10	15	16	19

GAUGE

Exact gauge is **essential** for proper size. Before beginning your project, make the sample swatch given in the individual instructions in the yarn and hook specified. After completing the swatch, measure it, counting your stitches and rows/rounds carefully. If your swatch is larger or smaller than specified, **make another, changing hook size to get the correct gauge**. Keep trying until you find the size hook that will give you the specified gauge.

MARKERS

Markers are used to help distinguish the beginning of each round being worked. Place a 2" (5 cm) scrap piece of yarn before the first stitch of each round, moving marker after each round is complete.

JOINING WITH DC

When instructed to join with dc, begin with a slip knot on hook. YO, holding loop on hook, insert hook in stitch or space indicated, YO and pull up a loop (3 loops on hook), (YO and draw through 2 loops on hook) twice.

JOINING WITH SC

When instructed to join with sc, begin with a slip knot on hook. Insert hook in stitch or space indicated, YO and pull up a loop, YO and draw through both loops on hook.

BACK OR FRONT LOOP ONLY

Work only in loop(s) indicated by arrow ***(Fig. 1)***.

Fig. 1

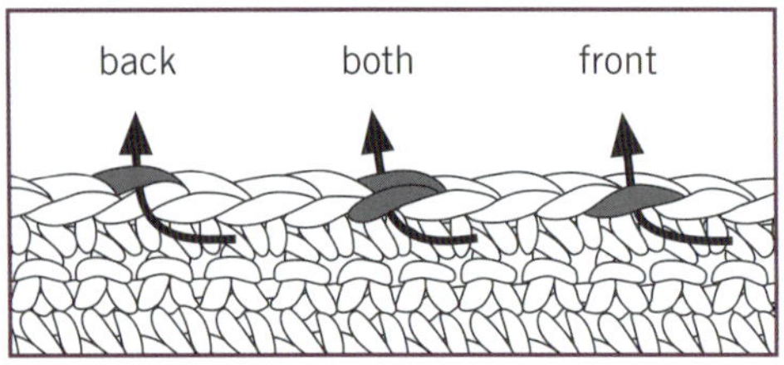

FREE LOOPS OF A CHAIN

When instructed to work in free loops of a chain, work in loop indicated by arrow ***(Fig. 2)***.

Fig. 2

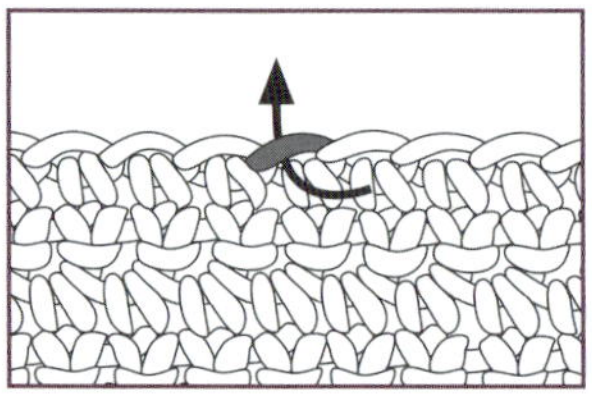

CHANGING COLORS

Work the last stitch to within one step of completion, hook new yarn ***(Fig. 3)*** and draw through all loops on hook. Cut old yarn and work over both ends.

Fig. 3

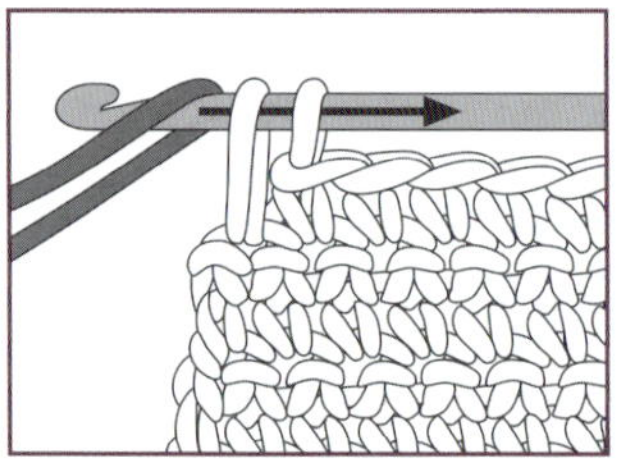

WHIPSTITCH

With **wrong** sides together, sew through both pieces once to secure the beginning of the seam, leaving an ample yarn end to weave in later. Insert the needle from **front** to **back** through one strand on each piece ***(Fig. 4)***. Bring the needle around and insert it from **front** to **back** through the next strand on both pieces.
Repeat along the edge, being careful to match stitches and rows.

Fig. 4

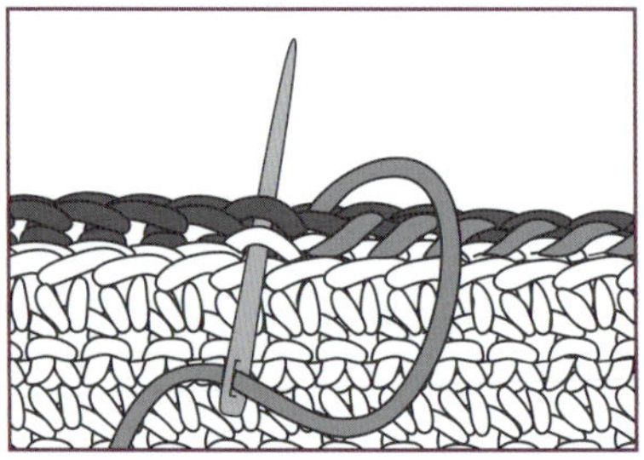

YARN INFORMATION

Projects in this leaflet were made using various weights of yarn. Any brand of the specified weight of yarn may be used. It is best to refer to the yardage/meters when determining how many balls or skeins to purchase. Remember, to arrive at the finished size, it is the GAUGE/TENSION that is important, not the brand of yarn. For your convenience, listed below are the specific yarns used to create our photography models.

MOBIUS COWL

Lion Brand® Babysoft®
#191 Violet

CHEMO CAPS

Red Heart® Boutique™ Fur Sure™
Men's - #9308 Camel
Women's - #9226 Magenta

BABY COMFORT BLANKET

Premier™ Yarns Deborah Norville Collection Everyday™ Soft Worsted Solids
Blue - # ED100-05 Baby Blue
Pink - #ED100-06 Baby Pink

KENNEL BLANKET

Red Heart® Soft Yarn
Tan - #9388 Wheat
Rust - #9275 Paprika
Green - #9522 Leaf
Orange - #4422 Tangerine
Blue - #9518 Teal

BABY HAT

Premier™ Yarns Deborah Norville Collection Everyday™ Soft Worsted Solids
#ED100-06 Baby Pink

COMFORTGHAN

Red Heart® Soft Yarn
Brown - #1882 Toast
Ecru - #4601 Off White
Variegated - #9935 Waterscape Print

PRAYER SHAWL

Lion Brand® Vanna's Choice®
Green Variegated - #304 Seaspray Mist
Lion Brand® Nature's Choice Organic® Cotton
Lt Green - #169 Dusty Sage
Tan - #123 Khaki
Cream - #098 Almond
Lion Brand® Homespun®
Blue - #341 Windsor
Purple - #336 Barrington
Lion Brand® Fun Fur
Ecru - #124 Champagne
Lion Brand® Wool-Ease® Thick & Quick®
Wine - #146 Fig

COMFORT TEDDY

Premier™ Yarns Deborah Norville Collection Serenity Sock Weight Solids
Brown - #DN150-06 Deep Brown
Cream - # DN150-01 Soft White

DRAWSTRING BAG

Lion Brand® Cotton-Ease®
Blue - #148 Turquoise
White - #100 Snow
Pink - #103 Blossom
Purple - #145 Plum
Green - #194 Lime
Dk Pink - #195 Azalea

NATIONAL ORGANIZATIONS

If you can't find a local resource to donate your crocheted goodies, here is a list of some national groups that would be happy to hear from you! Be sure to check with each organization before sending them a donation. They have their own set of guidelines that they have developed to make the experience satisfying for everyone.

BABY COMFORT BLANKET
Project Linus
www.projectlinus.org

BABY HAT
The Preemie Project
www.thepreemieproject.com

KENNEL BLANKET
Operation Blankets of Love
www.operationblanketsoflove.com

COMFORTGHAN
Heartmade Blessings
www.heartmadeblessings.org

CHEMO CAPS
Knots of Love®
www.knots-of-love.org

PRAYER SHAWL
Prayer Shawl Ministry
www.shawlministry.com

COMFORT TEDDY
Teddies for Tragedies
www.teddiesfortragedies.org

PRODUCTION TEAM

Instructional/Technical Editor: Sarah J. Green

Editorial Writer: Susan McManus Johnson

Graphic Artists: Becca Snider and Dana Vaughn

Senior Graphic Artist: Lora Puls

Photography Manager: Katherine Laughlin

Photo Stylists: Sondra Daniel and Brooke Duszota

Photographers: Ken West and Jason Masters